# The Story of Jeans

Lisa Klobuchar

*Photo Credits*

Tony Stone Images/Moggy, cover.

PhotoDisc, pages 1, 4, 4 inset, 21 insets.

Courtesy Levi Strauss & Co. Archives, San Francisco, CA,

pages 5, 8, 9, 11.

Tony Stone Images/Steven Weinberg, page 7.

Tony Stone Images/Hulton Getty, page13.

Corbis-Bettmann, page 14.

FPG International LLC/Willinger, page 15.

Phil Martin Photography, pages 16, 17, 18, 19, 20.

FPG International/Ron Chapple, page 21.


*Illustrations*

All illustrations by Garrian Manning.

Discovery World:

The Story of Jeans


©1998 Rigby

a division of Reed Elsevier Inc.

500 Coventry Lane

Crystal Lake, IL 60014

02 01 00

10 9 8 7 6 5 4 3 2


Printed in the United States of America

ISBN 0-7635-7229-2

Visit Rigby on the
World Wide Web at
http://www.rigby.com

# Contents

**Rigby**

# Popular Pants

People wear jeans almost everywhere. They wear them at home, at school, and at the movies. Many grown-ups wear jeans to work. It seems as if everybody wears jeans now. It wasn't always that way, though.

Long ago, only railroad workers, miners, and cowboys wore jeans. How did jeans get to be clothes that people wear all the time? It took almost one hundred years.

# Made of Denim

Jeans are pants with five pockets. They have two pockets in the front and two in the back. They also have one small pocket inside the right front pocket. This small pocket is called a watch pocket.

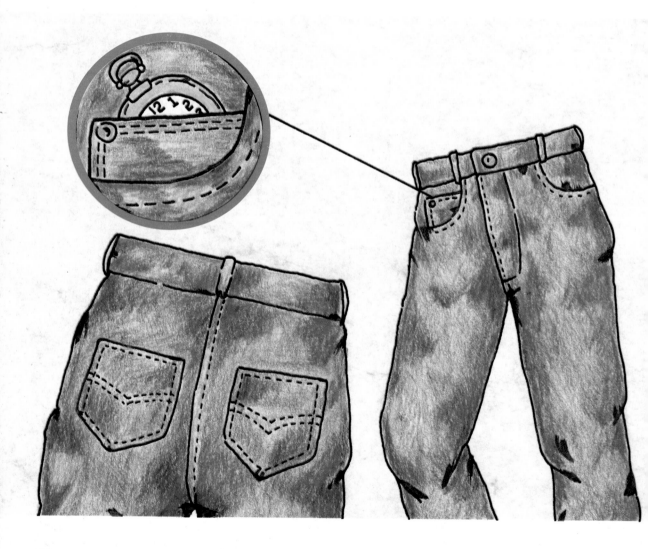

Most jeans are made of denim. Denim is a tough cotton cloth. Most denim for jeans is colored with a blue dye called indigo.

# The First Jeans

The first jeans were invented about 125 years ago by Jacob Davis and Levi Strauss. Jacob was a tailor in Reno, Nevada. He sewed sturdy work clothes to sell to miners, cowboys, and other workers. Levi owned a company that sold cloth, clothing, and other goods.

**Levi Strauss**

**1870**
**Jeans Time Line**

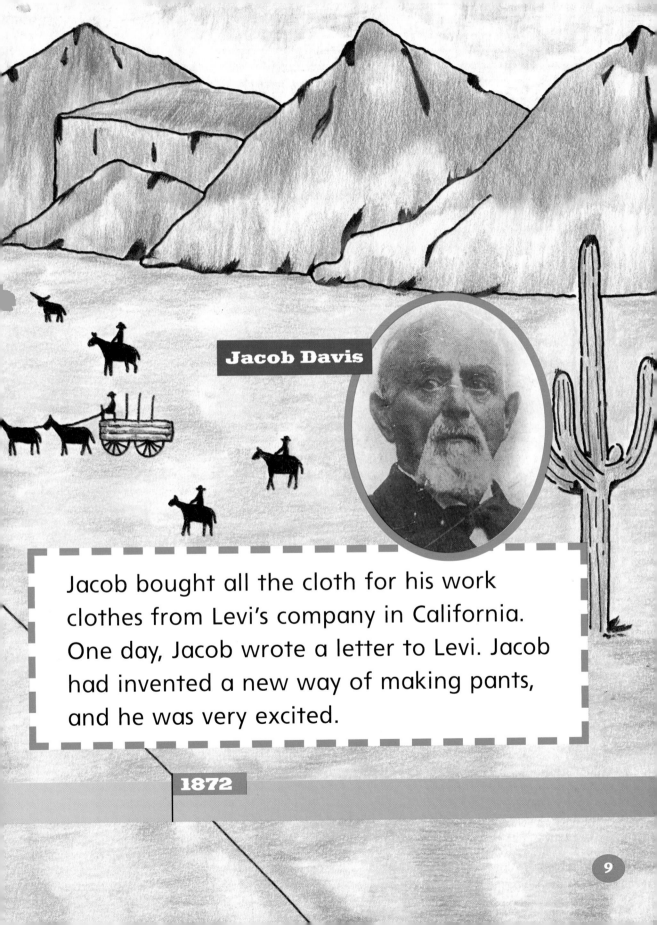

Jacob Davis

Jacob bought all the cloth for his work clothes from Levi's company in California. One day, Jacob wrote a letter to Levi. Jacob had invented a new way of making pants, and he was very excited.

1872

# Pants with Rivets

Jacob told Levi that he attached the pockets onto the pants with small metal bolts called rivets. The pockets didn't tear like they did on regular pants. Jacob said that his new kind of pants were so popular that he could not make them fast enough.

Jacob needed help. He asked Levi if he would be his partner. Levi knew a good idea when he heard one. He said yes right away. Soon the two men were making a fortune selling Jacob's rivet-pocket work pants.

1875

# Waist Overalls

Back then, the pants were not called jeans. Levi called the pants "waist overalls." Instead of a zipper, the pants had buttons. Instead of belt loops, the pants had buttons for suspenders.

**Then**

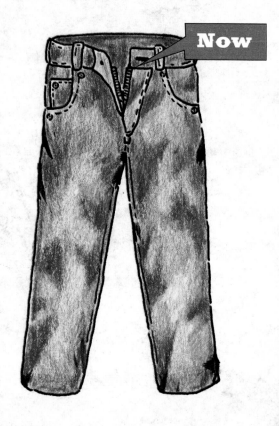

**Now**

**1890**

In the 1920s and 1930s, jeans started to become popular. People opened vacation spots called dude ranches in the western United States. People from the East Coast went there to ride horses and dress like cowboys. These people took jeans home with them.

1920

1930

# In the Movies

Then in the 1950s, Hollywood movies started to show young actors wearing jeans. Young people all over the United States thought these actors looked very cool. They wanted to dress like these movie stars.

1950

Most parents and teachers did not like seeing young people in jeans. Many schools had "no jeans" rules for students. At school girls wore dresses, and boys wore slacks. But after school, they couldn't wait to change into their jeans.

**1955**

# For Everyday

As time went by, more and more young people wore jeans. People began to think that wearing jeans was okay. In the early 1960s, there were only a few styles of jeans. They all had slim legs and most were dark blue.

1965

Then, about 1970, clothing makers began to offer styles such as hip huggers and bell bottoms.

1970

# Many Styles and Colors

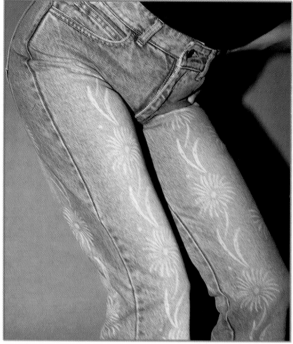

A few years later, designer jeans became popular. Designer jeans had many styles and colors. Sometimes they had fancy stitching. But these jeans were very tight. They cost a lot of money, too.

**1975**

People soon got tired of designer jeans.
They wanted comfortable jeans. Clothing
makers offered stone-washed jeans. These
jeans were washed with stones to fade
the color and make the cloth soft.

1980

People loved their old, worn-out jeans so much that torn jeans became stylish. Some clothing stores even sold jeans that were already torn.

1990

1995

In 1995, people all over the world bought more than 500 million pairs of jeans. Today, you can find baggy jeans, slim jeans, and jeans in a rainbow of colors. There is a style of jeans for everybody.

2000

# Time Line of Jeans

1970

1980

1995

# Index